Plant or Animal?

CONCEPT SCIENCE

Written by Judith Holloway and Clive Harper
Illustrated by Sandy Coulthart

Some living things are plants.

Most plants can't move about.
Most plants have roots which hold them in the ground.

Some living things are animals.
Animals **can** move about.

Some plants are so tiny
we can see them
only through a microscope.

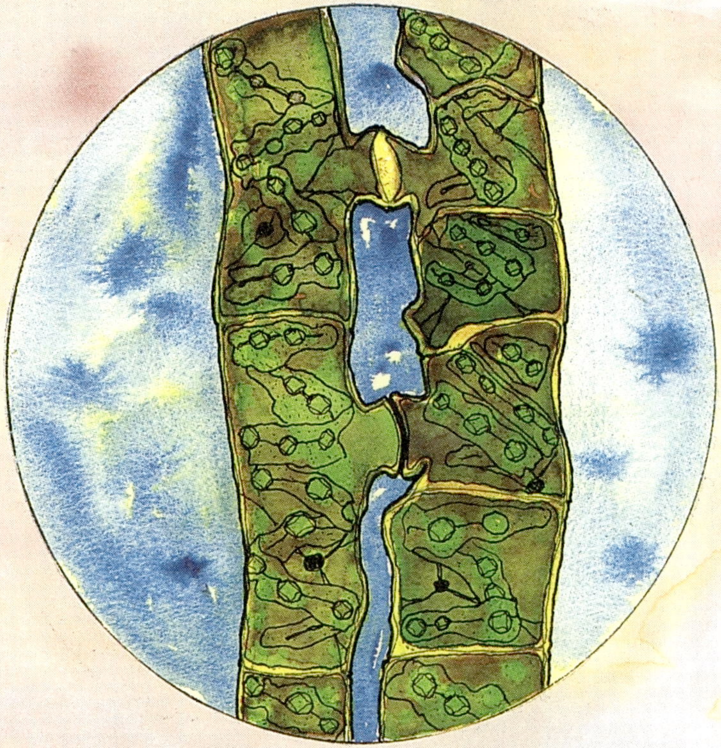

algae (enlarged 750,000 times)

Some animals are so tiny
we can see them
only through a miscroscope.

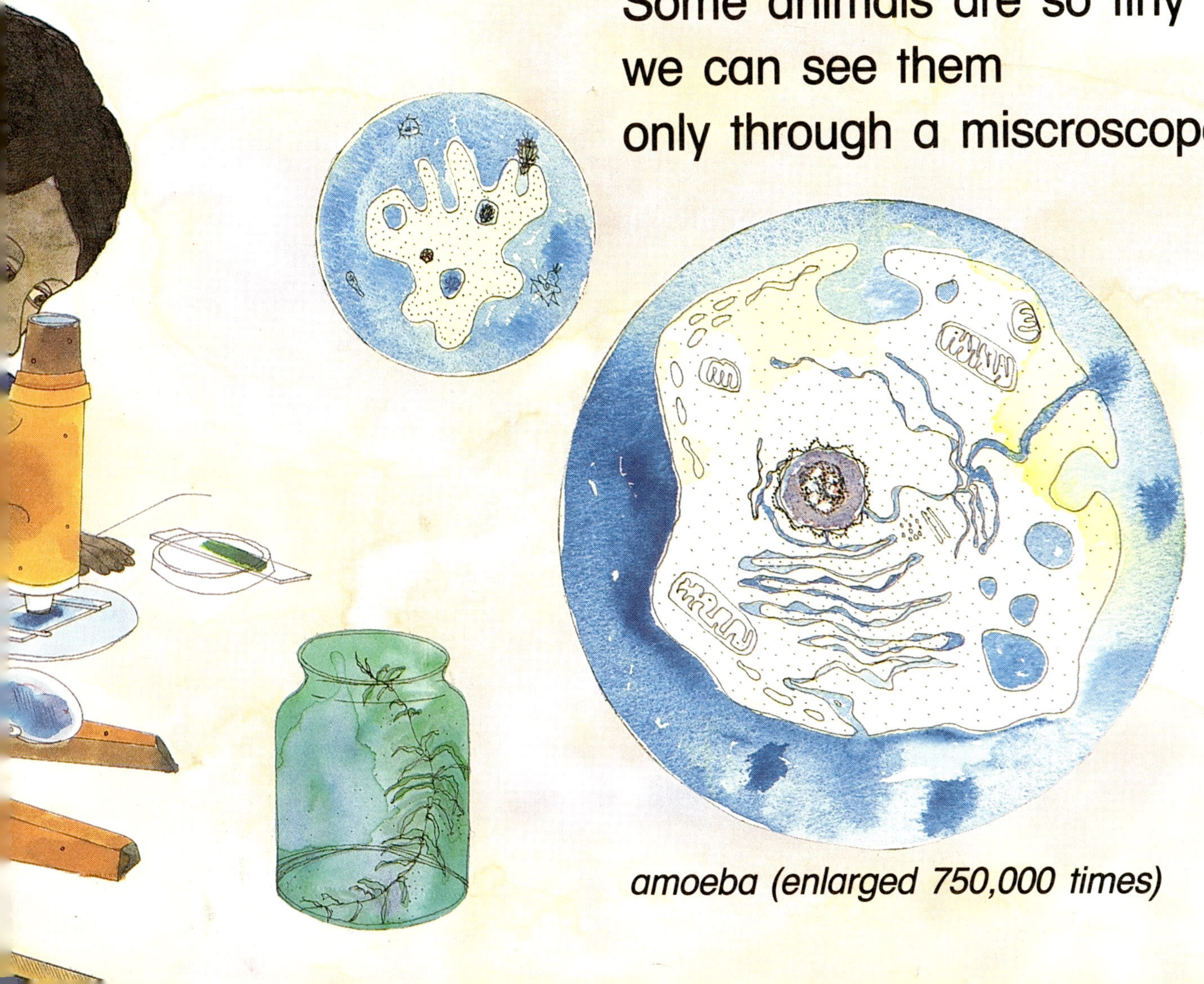

amoeba (enlarged 750,000 times)

QUIZ

See if you are right.
The answers are on Page 13.

1. Is a  an animal?

2. Is a  an animal?

3. Is a  an animal?

4. Is a 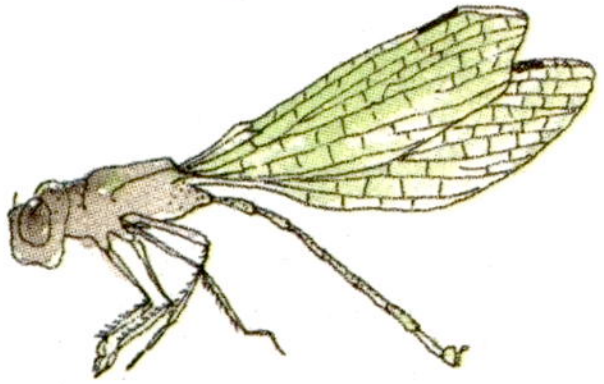 an animal?

5. Is a  an animal?

6. Is a 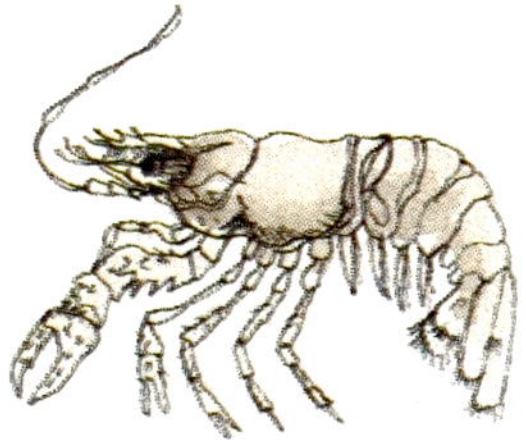 an animal?

7. Are  animals?

8. Are  animals?

9. Are  plants?

10. Is a  a plant?

11. Is a 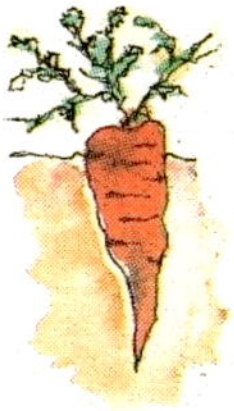 a plant?

12. Is a  a plant?

13. Are  plants?

14. Is a  a plant?

15. Is a  a plant?

Answers:

1. Yes
2. Yes
3. Yes
4. Yes
5. Yes
6. Yes
7. Yes
8. No
9. Yes
10. Yes
11. Yes
12. Yes
13. Yes
14. Yes
15. Yes

QUIZ

Ask your friend these questions. . .

Do  grow into animals or plants?

Do  grow into animals or plants?

Can all animals move about?

How does a  move about?

How does a  move about?

How does a  move about?

How does a 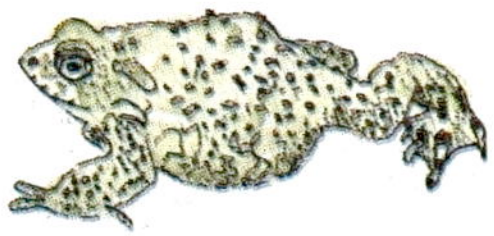 move about?

How does a  move about?

Which animal can run and hop and
climb and swim but cannot fly
by itself?

A human.

Some things for you to do by yourself or as a group

1. Draw an animal you love and a plant you love—both in the same picture.

Draw in all the things your plant and animal need to live.

Now write about all the other things you've found out about your plant and animal.

How do they take in air? How do they reproduce? What else can you find out?

2. Take a flower on a stem (a white flower would be best) and a stick of celery.

Place one in a glass of water and the other in a glass of half water and half ink.

Watch every day. What happens? Why does it happen?